Dried Flower Crafts

❖

*Capturing the
Best of Your Garden
to Decorate Your Home*

Art Direction: Dana Irwin
Production: Dana Irwin
Proofreading: Julie Brown
Illustrations: Alexander James, Kevin James

Library of Congress Cataloging-in-Publication Data

Cusick, Dawn.
    Dried flower crafts: capturing the best of your garden to
decorate your home / Dawn Cusick.
        p. cm.
    Includes index.
    ISBN 0-8069-6120-1
    1. Dried flower arrangement. 2. Nature Craft. I. Title.
SB449.3.D7C87 1996   95-44155
745.92--dc20   CIP

10 9 8 7 6 5 4 3 2 1

A Sterling/Lark Book

First paperback edition published in 1997 by
    Sterling Publishing Company, Inc.
        387 Park Avenue South, New York, N.Y. 10016

Produced by Altamont Press, Inc.
    50 College Street, Asheville, NC 28801

© 1996 by Altamont Press

Distributed in Canada by Sterling Publishing, % Canadian Manda Group
    One Atlantic Avenue, Suite 105, Toronto, Ontario, Canada M6K 3E7
Distributed in Great Britain and Europe by Cassell PLC
    Wellington House, 125 Strand, London WC2R 0BB, England
Distributed in Australia by Capricorn Link (Australia) Pty Ltd.
    P.O. Box 6651, Baulkham Hills, Business Centre, NSW 2153, Australia

Sterling ISBN 0-8069-6120-1 Trade
                0-8069-6121-X Paper

2

Dried Flower Crafts

❖

*Capturing the
Best of Your Garden
to Decorate Your Home*

Dawn Cusick

A Sterling /Lark Book

Sterling Publishing Co., Inc. New York

TABLE OF CONTENTS

INTRODUCTION

If you love fresh flowers, you will relish the opportunity to preserve the vibrance of their beauty with Dried Flower Crafts. Dried flowers are a cooperative and remarkably versatile crafting material. The intriguing nuances of their shapes and colors make boredom a near impossibility, and you will marvel at the remarkable similarities and differences in blooms when compared with their fresh-cut counterparts.

Crafters will approach the projects in this book with as many different working styles as there are personalities. Some crafters will putter through the projects in the same way they'd putter around in the garden, letting the flowers talk to

them as they work and using them as inspirations. Other crafters will choose to zip right through projects, replicating their designs as closely and quickly as possible. Any method that produces great results is a great choice. As you approach the projects, always feel free to delete or add flowers, depending on availability and personal preference. Before finalizing a substitution, study the original project carefully to see how the materials you plan to substitute were used, i.e. as background materials, accents, or as contributors to a well-established color scheme. Substituting materials with similar design functions will ensure successful results.

Enjoy your flowers.

TOOLS & TECHNIQUES

If you're new to dried flower crafting, the following descriptions of tools and techniques may seem intimidating. Actually, the basic tools and techniques can be mastered in an afternoon, and your confidence and skills will increase with the completion of each new project. Not every tool or technique is needed for every project, so after a brief skim of this chapter you may wish to choose a specific project before you purchase and practice with the materials.

❖ TOOLS ❖

GLUE GUNS

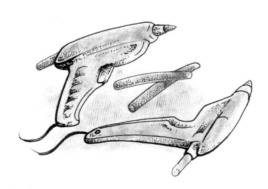

Glue guns come in a startling array of sizes, price ranges, and varieties. An inexpensive mini glue gun will get the job done, but a low-melt glue gun (less chance of painful burns) with an extra long or detachable cord is well worth the extra cost. Read through the manufacturer's instructions before beginning work and then do some practice gluing to get the feel of a glue gun.

FLORAL WIRE

Floral wire comes in a number of thicknesses — known as gauges — ranging from ultrathin to almost as thick as coat hanger wire. Choose a gauge that is sturdy enough to do the job, yet flexible enough to shape and twist.

Floral wire is frequently used to attach materials to a base when you want to play with placement angles or when an item is too heavy to attach with just hot glue. To wire an item to a base, first cut a length of flexible floral wire to 12 inches (30 cm). Look for an inconspicuous place on your item. When you're wiring bows, for example, you can slip the wire through the center loop and it will not show in the finished project. If no such place exists, give some thought as to what you can use to cover up the wire once it's in place. A small length of ribbon, perhaps, or a few sprigs of green-

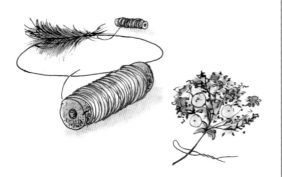

Floral tape comes in a variety of colors and widths, and is used to add strength, to cover wire, or to create a smoother surface. For best results, stretch the tape slightly as you work and apply it at an angle.

FLORAL PICKS

These short wooden picks come with a length of thin-gauge wire at the top end and an angled tip at the bottom. They are used as a time-saving assembly technique

ery should do the trick. Center the wire on the item and twist both ends together, then hold the item tightly against the base and again twist the wires together.

FLORAL PINS

Also known as u-pins and greening pins, these curved pieces of wire look and work like old-fashioned hairpins. To use one, position your materials against a straw or foam base. Center the pin's prongs over the materials and press the pin into the base at an angle.

FLORAL TAPE

and/or to prevent delicate stems from breaking. The wire secures small bouquets of flowers together so they can be attached to a base as one piece instead of as five or six individual pieces, and the stems can be wrapped with floral tape. The bouquets can contain only one variety of blooms or any pleasing combination.

To work with a floral pick, first arrange a

grouping of materials into a small bouquet. The number of stems in the bouquets should be determined by their combined thickness. Some stems are so thin that you can get eight or nine stems on a pick and it still inserts easily into a straw or foam base; most others are thick enough to limit you to three to five stems. When you've fin-

ished arranging the stems, trim them even at the bottom.

Hold the bouquet with the stems pressed together near the midpoint of the pick, double-checking to make sure that the blooms protrude above the pick. Make several wraps around the stems with the wire in the same place, then spiral the wire down the pick.

For added durability and easier insertion into dense bases, picked bouquets should be wrapped with floral tape. Hold the tape just under the blooms at a slight angle and gently stretch the tape, then spiral the tape down the pick at an angle. When you reach the end of the pick, cut the tape and roll the cut end between your fingers to seal.

FLORAL FOAM

Floral foam (also known as craft foam) comes in any number of sizes, shapes, and colors. If you can't find the exact size or shape you want, just purchase the foam in a large block and cut it down to size with a serrated kitchen knife. Foam bases should be covered before using. A few handfuls of moss attached with floral pins and/or hot glue usually do the trick. Sturdy stems can be cut at an angle and inserted directly into the foam, while flowers with weaker stems should be picked or wired first.

RIBBONS

Each variety of ribbon has a distinct personality. Satin ribbon's strength is that it comes in so many widths that it's easy to find one to make the perfect size bow for your project. Paper ribbon is easy to reshape if you don't like the finished look of your bow. Cotton ribbon, similarly, can be ironed if you're not happy with your finished bow. For festive occasions, cellophane ribbon adds instant party glitz and is easy for beginners to work with. Raffia adds a natural touch to projects, is easy to work with, and takes dyes well.

Lace ribbon is ideal in wedding and Victorian projects; dip the lace in fabric stiffener before tying to help the bow loops hold their shape. Velvet ribbon adds an elegant touch to any bow, but can be difficult for beginners to work with. Finally, there's French ribbon (sometimes called wired ribbon), which comes with rows of thin-gauge wire on the wrong side to help create loops and bows that stay where you put them. Ribbons can also be used to cover an unsightly wreath base. Just wrap the ribbon around the base at an angle and secure with sewing or greening pins.

FLOWERS

If you plan to purchase your blooms, take a few minutes to analyze your proposed project. Does it contain a variety of blooms or is there a single background flower? Do you need an equal amount of assorted blooms or a large amount of a single background material and then just a few accent blooms. Blooms can be expensive to purchase, and many of the inexpensive imported blooms found in large craft stores have been treated with dyes and pesticides, diluting their natural beauty. Your local florist may have a good selection of choice blooms.

SILK FLOWERS

Although silks have been scorned by many nature crafters, they are often the perfect choice for accent flowers or as background or filler material. When shopping for silks, keep in mind that a single stem can be cut down into several smaller stems or into individual blooms. The large difference in price ranges often correlates with large difference in appearance and quality, so try to avoid dime-store silks if a professional-quality arrangement is what you're after.

❖ TECHNIQUES ❖

ARRANGEMENTS

The first step to making an arrangement is to choose an interesting container. Cut a piece of foam to fit snugly inside the container and add rocks or fishing weights to increase stability if necessary. Cover the top and any protruding sides of the foam with moss. Tough-stemmed blooms such as yarrow can be cut at an angle and inserted directly into the foam. Easily broken stems should be attached to a floral pick and wrapped with floral tape.

Give some thought about the overall shape you'd like for the arrangement before you begin inserting materials. The shape should complement the container and the location where you plan to display it, as well as be compatible with the stem lengths of the floral materials you have available. For beginners, oval, triangular, and round shapes

tend to yield the best results. Establish the outer boundaries first and then fill in the remainder of the arrangement, adding the heaviest, most sturdy materials first and saving the lighter, more delicate materials for last.

GARLANDS AND SWAGS

Garlands and swags are the perfect way to add the beauty of dried flowers to special places around your home. They can be custom-designed to fit special areas, such as over a mirror or across a dresser top or mantel. A garland can be formed over any base that's strong enough to support the materials and flexible enough to allow the finished garland to drape in graceful curves. Macrame cord and heavy-gauge floral wire are popular base choices.

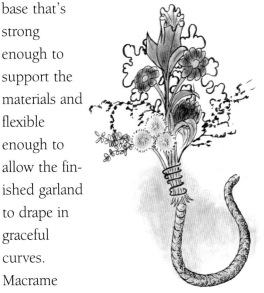

To make a garland, measure the area where you plan to display it and cut a base to this

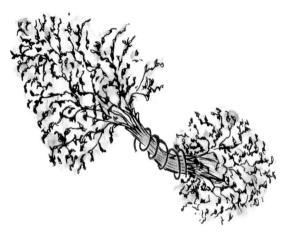

length plus 12 inches (30 cm). Arrange your dried flower materials in small bouquets of four to eight stems. The bouquets can contain just one material or they can be a mix of several different blooms. Wire the stems of each bouquet together with fine-gauge wire. Then wire the bunches to the base, taking care to position each new bouquet so that it covers the stems of the previous bouquet. For a delicate garland, wire all of the bunches facing the same direction; for a fluffier garland, alternately tilt each one slightly to the left, to the right, and then straight on. Another option is to work from the center point outward to each end, then go back to the center and cover the center gap with a large bow.

HANGING BOUQUETS

These decorative wall pieces are simply large bouquets of dried materials designed to hang vertically. First arrange the bouquet in a fan shape and secure the stems about

4 inches (10 cm) up from the stems' ends with floral wire. Cover the wire with several ties of ribbon or a large bow. Extra accents, such as cones, pods, mosses, or single blooms of flowers can then be tied into the bouquet.

WREATHS

The basic process of making a wreath is simple. Divide the wreath base into three imaginary sections: the outer edge, the inner edge, and the center surface. When working with picked bouquets, be sure to insert each bouquet at the same angle to create a clear, circular line around the base. Each new bouquet should be positioned to cover the stems of the previous bouquet, and the stems from the last bouquet should be tucked neatly under the foliage of the first bouquet to make the starting and ending points indistinguishable. Single accent blooms can be hot-glued into the picked materials, or an entire wreath base can be covered with individual blooms.

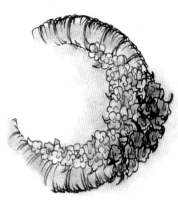

A fun variety of wreath bases can be found in most large craft stores, each with its own set of benefits and drawbacks. Vine bases are an all-around good choice for several reasons. The natural vine is so attractive that designers often leave large portions of the vine uncovered, and the vine makes a good adhesion surface for hot glue.

Vine bases are easy to make if you have access to fresh vines. Just curve four to six vines into a circle, allowing them to overlap about 2 inches. Wrap one or two longer vines around the circle to hold the first circle of vines in place. Vines that are not fresh-cut may need to be soaked first in a tub of warm water for softening. If you're custom-making a wreath for a specific location, vine is a good base choice because even the largest ones are relatively lightweight.

Straw bases create the lush, full wreaths that many people associate with expensive, professionally made wreaths. The straw bases available in craft stores are often covered with a layer of green plastic. If you're prone to allergies, leave the plastic on and insert picked bouquets of materials right through the plastic. otherwise, simply remove the plastic and throw it away. To prevent the stems of dried flowers from breaking when inserting them into dense straw, attach them first to floral picks. Be forewarned: it takes a lot of materials to cover a straw base, so you may wish to search out some inexpensive filler materials if you don't have a lot of dried flowers.

For a thin, delicate wreath, choose a wire ring base. These bases are ideal when working with wispy materials such as stems of

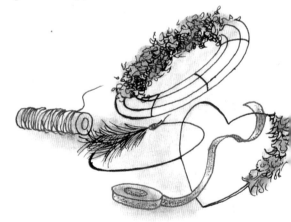

pussy willow and baby's-breath. They are not a good choice when you're working with larger items or when you plan to add heavy materials. Wire bases are also available with multiple wire rings positioned at different depths, creating a circular trench that can be filled with moss, pine needles, or fragrant flowers. Secure the materials in the trench by wrapping around the trench in even intervals with fishing wire or a compatible color of quilting thread. Single leaves or flower blooms can then be hot-glued on top of the natural materials; stems can be dabbed with glue and inserted into the base material.

Foam bases are another versatile option. Before you begin adding flowers, cover the foam surface with ribbon, fabric strips, or moss to prevent the foam from showing through in the finished wreath. Foam surfaces can also be sculpted with a serrated knife into interesting layers and then decorated with individual flowers.

Larger craft stores often feature interesting variations of traditional wreath bases, such as cinnamon-covered bases, mirror-centered bases, and bases with small shelves built in.

TOPIARIES

Craft topiaries are one of those fun crafts that can be as simple or complicated as you like. A topiary's basic anatomy consists of a flower pot, a sturdy stem, and a foam ball. With these basic pieces you can create

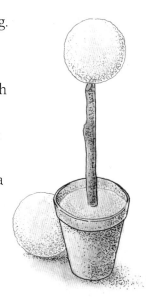

virtually anything. The flower pot can be painted or decorated with dried   flowers. The stem can be made from a wooden dowel, a cinnamon stick, or any naturally attractive find from the woods. More than one ball can be used to create double or even triple topiaries. Ribbon can be looped down the stem and tied in a bow at the bottom. (French wire ribbons are especially easy to work with and attractive.) Helpful tips: Add fishing weights to the bottom of the pot to increase stability if needed; to attach blooms with stems to the topiary's foam ball, press the tip of a pencil into the foam to make a small hole, then glue the stem into the hole for a more   natural look.

POTPOURRIS

A potpourri can be anything you want it to be: a bowl of pretty blooms with no fragrance, the same bowl of flowers plus a few wood shavings that have been soaked in a fragrant essential oil, or it can be a traditional potpourri made with interesting fragrance combinations and "fixed" with a fixative such as orrisroot, gum benzoin resin, tonka beans, vetiver root, sandalwood bark, or patchouli leaves.

To make a traditional potpourri, create a fragrance base from scented materials such as roses, scented geraniums, honeysuckle, lavender, rosemary, allspice, cinnamon, star anise, nutmeg, cloves, lemon verbena, lemon balm, lemon basil, or citrus peels, just to name a few. When you're happy with the base fragrance, add some dried blooms and leaves to make it look pretty. For each cup of potpourri, sprinkle about 1 tablespoon of fixative over the dried materials. If you want to intensify the fragrance with an essential oil, now is the time to add a few drops. Mix the potpourri well with a wooden spoon and place it in a paper bag. Roll the bag up tightly so there's no extra air and shake well, then place the bag in a dark location and shake once a day for a week; for the next five weeks, shake the bag once a week, then enjoy.

BOWS

The right bow can transform an average-looking project into an extraordinary one. The wide range of ribbon colors, patterns, and textures available — from paisleys to polka dots, pastels to brights, raffia to velvet — enables you to create just the right style.

A bow is simply a symmetrical arrangement of ribbon loops that's embellished with streamers. The number and size of the loops and the width of the ribbon determine the bow's finished look. Learning to tie a bow is a simple process, but it takes practice to achieve professional results.

To make a bow, first cut an 8-inch length (20 cm) of ribbon at an angle to form the first two streamers. Crimp the middle of the streamer and hold it tightly between your thumb and index finger. Then make a third streamer by crimping an uncut length of ribbon about 4 inches from one end.

Holding the streamers tightly, form a medium-size loop (about 3 to 4 inches, 7-1/2 to 10 cm), making sure the right side of the ribbon is facing outward. (Note: A loop consists of two parts, a top loop and a bottom loop.) Now make another medium-size loop, positioning it so it's next to the previous loop and not on top of it. Be careful to keep the center tightly crimped.

Form two larger loops about an inch longer than the medium-size loops. Now create two smaller loops about an inch smaller than the medium-size loops and position them on top of the large loops. Add two more medium-size loops adjacent to the large loops.

Switch the bow to your other hand, holding tightly to prevent your work from unraveling. Twist a length of thin-gauge floral wire around the streamers and the loops. Trim the uncut length of ribbon to match the of the other streamers.

Cover the wire with a short length of ribbon looped around the center and hot-glued in place on the back side. Fluff and shape the bow by pulling the streamers and rolling your finger around the inside of the loops in the order in which they were added.

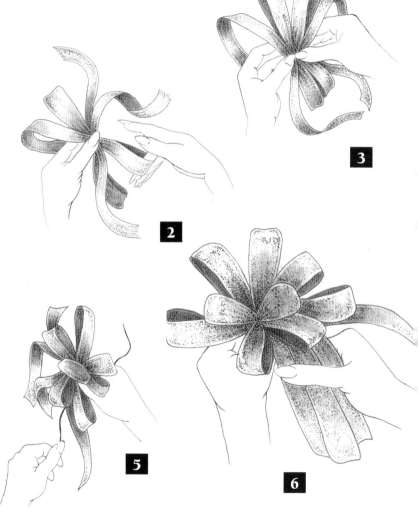

WREATHS

OVAL WREATH

❖

Oval-shaped bases allow crafters to create wreaths with interior design considerations in mind. (Vertically positioned ovals look especially nice on doors, while horizontals work well on long walls.) To make the wreath, attach small bouquets of sweet Annie and preserved fern to floral picks, then hot-glue the picks into an oval wreath base. Arrange a long length of French ribbon into a bow with curved streamers and hot-glue it to the center top of the wreath. Finish by hot-gluing single blooms and stems of strawflowers, dahlias, zinnias, beebalm, love-in-a-mist, salvia Victoria, Mexican bush sage, and assorted pods into the sweet Annie.

DESIGNER
DIANE WEAVER

Hydrangea Heart

❖❖❖

Large stems of hydrangea blooms make an ideal filler material for large, lush wreaths. To make this wreath, hot-glue a large bow and curving streamers to the center top of a heart-shaped peppergrass wreath base. Separate the hydrangea clusters into smaller sections and hot-glue them around the top and sides of the base. Finish by hot-gluing stems and single blooms of larkspur, carnations, roses, strawflowers, common immortelle, love-in-a-mist, and lemon leaves.

Designer
Kim Tibbals

WREATH
CENTERPIECE
❖

VIRTUALLY ANY WALL WREATH
CAN BE DISPLAYED ON A TABLE
AS A CENTERPIECE, AND THE
CENTER HOLE MAKES A
CONVENIENT PLACE FOR A
LARGE CANDLE. TO MAKE THE
WREATH, PICK SMALL BOUQUETS
OF GERMAN STATICE INTO A
STRAW WREATH BASE, THEN
HOT-GLUE CONEFLOWERS,
ZINNIAS, STRAWFLOWERS,
GLOBE AMARANTH,
LOVE-IN-A-MIST, FEVERFEW,
AND CHAMOMILE INTO
THE STATICE.

DESIGNER
DOLLY LUTZ MORRIS

SILVER AND GOLD WREATH

❖

T HE BRIGHT BEAUTY OF THIS LUSH WREATH COMES FROM BEAUTIFUL GOLD AND SILVER BLOOM AND FOLIAGE CHOICES. TO MAKE THE WREATH, FORM A BACKGROUND OF SILVER-KING ARTEMISIA BY ATTACHING SMALL BUNDLES TO FLORAL PICKS AND THEN HOT-GLUING THE PICKS INTO A VINE BASE. FINISH BY HOT-GLU-ING BILLY BUTTONS, MARIGOLDS, ANNUAL STA-TICE, GLOBE AMARANTH, MONKEY PAWS, AND SAGO INTO THE ARTEMISIA.

DESIGNER
DIANE WEAVER

HEART WREATH

❖

SMALL, HEART-SHAPED WREATHS CAN BE CRE-
ATED INEXPENSIVELY FROM VINE BASES AND
GARDEN FLOWERS, AND MAKE MEMORABLE
ALTERNATIVES TO GREETING CARDS. TO MAKE
THE WREATH, HOT-GLUE LEMON TREE LEAVES
AROUND THE OUTSIDE EDGE OF THE BASE,
THEN COVER THE REMAINING SURFACE AREA
WITH LARKSPUR, DAISIES, GLOBE AMARANTH,
BABY EVERLASTINGS, ROSES, DAFFODILS, AND
BABY'S BREATH.

DESIGNER
DIANE WEAVER

BRIGHT SUMMER WREATH

❖

A MELANGE OF PURPLE, RED, AND PINK BLOOMS CREATES THIS COLORFUL HARVEST OF SUMMER COLOR. TO MAKE THE WREATH, HOT-GLUE SHORT STEMS OF PRESERVED FERN AROUND A TWIG BASE. FINISH BY HOT-GLUING SINGLE BLOOMS OF STRAWFLOWERS, ROSES, STATICE, ZINNIAS, GLOBE AMARANTH, AND SEED HYACINTH TO THE BASE.

DESIGNER
KIM TIBBALS

28

ROSE AND LARKSPUR WREATH

❖

The swirling branches of this sweet huck base enhance the charm of its miniature size. To make the wreath, hot-glue sheet moss around the inside of the base to create a natural-looking design surface. Arrange small bunches of larkspur and rosebuds in groups of five and hot-glue them to the moss in an alternating pattern.

DESIGNER
JOAN NAYLOR

MUSHROOM WREATH

❖

A SWEET HUCK WREATH BASE AND LARGE DRIED MUSHROOMS FORM A NATURALLY CONTRASTING BACKGROUND FOR DELICATE DRIED FLOWERS. TO MAKE THE WREATH, HOT-GLUE THIN STRIPS OF SHEET MOSS AROUND THE EDGE OF THE WREATH. POSITION AND HOT-GLUE THE MUSHROOMS AROUND THE WREATH, THEN HOT-GLUE SMALL GROUPINGS OF ROSES, AMBROSIA, POPPY PODS, ZINNIAS, QUEEN-ANNE'S-LACE, BUTTERFLY BUSH, VERONICA, PRINCESS FEATHER, AND DELPHINIUM IN THE SPACES BETWEEN THE MUSHROOMS.

DESIGNER
JOAN NAYLOR

INVITING
WREATH

❖

HUES OF GOLD, WHITE, AND GREEN BLEND
TOGETHER TO FORM AN INVITING WREATH. TO
MAKE THE WREATH, ATTACH SMALL BOUQUETS
OF SWEET ANNIE TO FLORAL PICKS. GLUE THE
PICKS INTO A GRAPEVINE WREATH BASE, WORK-
ING FIRST ON THE OUTER EDGE, THEN THE
INNER EDGE, AND THEN THE CENTER AREA.
FINISH BY HOT-GLUING INDIVIDUAL BLOOMS
OF SUNFLOWERS, KANGAROO-PAWS,
STRAWFLOWERS, ANNUAL STATICE, DAISIES,
YARROW, AND HYDRANGA INTO THE SWEET
ANNIE.

DESIGNER
DIANE WEAVER

BABY'S BREATH WHIMSY

❖

THE WHIMSICAL LOOK OF DRIED BABY'S-BREATH CREATES A DELICATE BACKGROUND FOR A POTPOURRI OF DRIED GARDEN FLOWERS. TO MAKE THE WREATH, ATTACH SMALL BOUQUETS OF BABY'S-BREATH TO FLORAL PICKS AND HOT-GLUE THE PICKS INTO A STRAW WREATH BASE, WORKING FIRST AROUND THE OUTER EDGE, THEN THE INNER EDGE, AND FINALLY IN THE CENTER AREA. NEXT, HOT-GLUE INDIVIDUAL BLOOMS OF HYDRANGEA, ANNUAL STATICE, GLOBE AMARANTH, ZINNIAS, NIGELLA, XERAN-THIUM, LARKSPUR, AND STRAWFLOWERS INTO THE BABY'S-BREATH. FINISH BY HOT-GLUING SEVERAL SILK MUSHROOMS AND OTHER FUNGI TO THE CENTER BOTTOM OF THE WREATH.

DESIGNER
DIANE WEAVER

TAPESTRY WREATH

❖

A TAPESTRY-PRINT BOW BLENDS SHADES OF
GREY, IVORY, AND PINK BLOOMS INTO A TRULY
ENCHANTING WREATH. TO MAKE THE WREATH,
WIRE SMALL BOUQUETS OF SILVER-KING
ARTEMISIA TO A WIRE BASE, THEN HOT-GLUE
INDIVIDUAL BLOOMS OF HYDRANGEA,
STRAWFLOWERS, ZINNIAS, GLOBE AMARANTH,
AND ROSES INTO THE ARTEMISIA. ARRANGE
AND HOT-GLUE INDIVIDUAL STEMS OF LATEX
LEAVES AND ARTEMISIA AROUND THE WREATH,
THEN FINISH WITH A BOW.

DESIGNER
DIANE WEAVER

FRAGRANT WREATH

❖

An enchanting assortment of flowers in shades of pink and white form a lovely contrast against a background of fragrant sweet Annie. To make the wreath, secure small bouquets of sweet Annie to floral picks and hot-glue the picks around the inner and outer edges of a grapevine wreath base. Fill in the middle area by hot-gluing single blooms of roses, hydrangea, baby's-breath, daisies, strawflowers, lavender, and annual statice to the base, then finish with a large French ribbon bow.

DESIGNER
DIANE WEAVER

SIMPLE WREATH

❖

THIS HANDSOME WREATH CONTRASTS WON-
DERFULLY WITH MOST NATURAL WOODS, MAK-
ING IT AN IDEAL WALL PIECE FOR PANELED OR
HEAVILY WOODED ROOMS. TO MAKE THE
WREATH, ATTACH BUNDLES OF PRESERVED FERN
AND SWEET ANNIE TO FLORAL PICKS AND THEN
HOT-GLUE THE PICKS INTO A VINE WREATH
BASE. ADD COLOR TO THE BACKGROUND BY
HOT-GLUING CARNATIONS, GLOBE AMARANTH,
SAGO, LARKSPUR, MEXICAN SAGE, AND AGAPAN-
THUS INTO THE BACKGROUND MATERIALS.

DESIGNER
DIANE WEAVER

TOPIARIES
GARLANDS, &
SWAGS

ASPARAGUS FERN ARCH

❖

Wispy stems of asparagus fern and caspia create a romantic tone for this piece. To make the arch, twist three lengths of floral wire together and curve them in an arch. Create small bouquets with three stems of asparagus fern with one lamb's-ear and two stems of dusty-miller and secure them together with floral tape. Wrap the pick's base with floral wire and then tape it to the wire base. (Work from one end in toward the center and then repeat for the other end.) Hot-glue blooms of statice, miniature roses, heather, lavender, yarrow, celosia, and sea lavender into the greenery, then loosely weave a translucent ribbon around the arch, hot-gluing as needed on the back side.

DESIGNER
KIM TIBBALS

BLOOMING VINE SWAG

❖

Inexpensive, flat vine bases come in an interesting variety of shapes and can easily be adapted to any number of craft projects. To prepare the base, cut out a sheet of cardboard that's slightly smaller than a flat vine base and hot-glue it to the top of the base. Cover the cardboard with moss, then begin hot-gluing blooms in place, working first with dahlias, then globe amaranth, then hydrangea, zinnias, larkspur, Queen-Anne's-lace, annual statice, helipterium, and finally the pansies. Additional accent pieces, such as small birds or butterflies, should be added last.

DESIGNER
JOAN NAYLOR

QUICK TOPIARIES

❖

CRAFT STORES OFTEN OFFER AN INTERESTING VARIETY OF PREMADE TOPIARY FORMS THAT ALLOW YOU TO START AND FINISH A TOPIARY IN LESS TIME THAN IT TAKES TO DO A LOAD OF LAUNDRY. YOU CAN HOT-GLUE ON JUST A FEW OF YOUR FAVORITE FLOWER SPRIGS, LEAVING PART OF THE BASE TO SHOW THROUGH, OR YOU CAN COVER THE FORM WITH A LUSH SELECTION OF BLOOMS. TO MAKE THE TOPIARY SHOWN HERE, TRIM SEVERAL LARGE STEMS OF GERMAN STATICE AND PEPPERBERRIES DOWN TO 2- AND 3-INCH LENGTHS (5 AND 7.5 CM), THEN HOT-GLUE THEM TO THE BALL FORMS AND AROUND THE BOTTOM OF THE POT. FINISH BY HOT-GLUING GLOBE AMARANTH BLOOMS THROUGHOUT THE STATICE AND BERRIES.

DESIGNER
CYNTHIA GILLOOLY

BIRDHOUSE BOUQUETS

❖

ANYONE WHO CAN POSITION A NAIL AND SWING A HAMMER CAN CREATE AN INTERESTING BASE FOR STUNNING ARRANGEMENTS. TO CREATE A BASE, SEARCH OUT SEVERAL STURDY BRANCHES AT LEAST 1-INCH THICK (2.5 CM) AND WITH INTERESTING SHAPES. NAIL ONE OF THE BRANCHES TO AN 8- TO 12-INCH (20 TO 30 CM) SQUARE OF PLYWOOD AND THEN NAIL A LIGHTWEIGHT BIRDHOUSE TO THE TOP END OF THE BRANCH. CUT A SQUARE OF 1-INCH-THICK FOAM SEVERAL INCHES SMALLER THAN THE PLYWOOD BASE, GLUE IT TO THE PLYWOOD, AND COVER THE FOAM WITH MOSS USING HOT GLUE AND FLORAL PINS. NAIL SEVERAL SMALLER BRANCHES UNDER THE PLYWOOD BASE AND TO THE BIRDHOUSE FOR A MORE NATURAL LOOK.

TO MAKE THE SMALLER BIRD-HOUSE ARRANGEMENT, PICK AND HOT-GLUE GERMAN STATICE, GLOBE AMARANTH, ANNUAL STA-TICE, ROSES, HEATHER, AND CELOSIA INTO THE BASE AND TO THE BIRDHOUSE.

TO MAKE THE LARGER BIRDHOUSE, HOT-GLUE A SHEET OF FOAM TO A RAFTLIKE SQUARE MADE FROM TRIMMED BRANCHES (A SHEET OF PLYWOOD MAY BE SUBSTITUTED). PICK STEMS OF GERMAN

STATICE, ANNUAL STATICE, PRE-
SERVED PLUMOSA FERN, IVY,
CASPIA, AND TI TREE INTO THE
BASE AND AROUND THE BIRD-
HOUSE. FOR ADDED DIMEN-
SION, GLUE A LARGE FOAM
BALL INTO ONE OF THE
BRANCHES AND THEN DECO-
RATE THE BALL WITH BLOOMS.
TO FINISH, ARRANGE AND HOT-
GLUE DRIED ORANGE SLICES
AND LOOPS OF A COORDINAT-
ING RIBBON INTO THE
ARRANGEMENT.

DESIGNER
CYNTHIA GILLOOLY

DECORATOR TOPIARY

❖

Naturally curly willow branches, a classic brass pot, and two colors of French ribbon add a decorator look to this simple topiary. To make the topiary, first cut a piece of foam to fit inside your container and then hot-glue it in place. Trim several willow branches to a length you find attractive.(1 to 2 feet, .3 to .6 m, is recommended.) Hot-glue the bottom of the branches into the foam base and the top branch into a large foam ball. Cover the base and ball forms with moss, and then begin hot-gluing roses, German statice, hydrangea, silk crab apples, and silk ivy into the moss on both the ball and the base. Finish by curving two colors of French ribbon through the willow branches and around the top of the ball, securing the ribbon in place on the ball with floral pins as needed.

DESIGNER
Cynthia Gillooly

SWEET ANNIE GARLAND

❖

THE BASE FOR THIS GARLAND WAS MADE FROM SWEET ANNIE, A FRAGRANT HERB WITH A WISPY, DELICATE APPEARANCE. TO MAKE THE GARLAND, BEGIN BY BRAIDING A BASE OF RAFFIA. (FOR A STURDIER GARLAND, BRAID THE RAFFIA WITH A LENGTH OF WIRE IN EACH STRAND OR LINE THE FINISHED BRAID WITH SEVERAL ROWS OF WIRE.) TRIM THE SWEET ANNIE TO 5-INCH (12 CM) LENGTHS, ARRANGE THEM IN THREE-STEM GROUPINGS, AND SECURE THE STEMS TOGETHER WITH FLORAL WIRE. FORM A BACKGROUND OF SWEET ANNIE BY HOT-GLUING THE STEMS INTO THE BRAID. NEXT, HOT-GLUE BLOOMS OF LEMON BALM BLOOMS, LOVE-IN-A-MIST, BLUE SALVIA, GLOBE AMARANTH, FEVERFEW, AND MINI POPPIES INTO THE SWEET ANNIE. FINISH BY HOT-GLUING CURVING STEMS OF AMARANTH THROUGHOUT THE GARLAND.

DESIGNER
KIM TIBBALS

ROSE AND LARKSPUR SWAGS

❖

Artificial pine swags are an excellent base choice for showcasing special flowers, and strategic flower positioning creates a more natural, three-dimensional look. To make a swag, first prepare the base by fluffing and shaping the branches. Attach your flowers and foliage into the pine with a glue gun, beginning on one side and working across to the other side. Place some materials under the front and in back of the base to create the attractive, three-dimensional look, and concentrate smaller materials in the center area and the larger ones on the top and sides of the swag.

For the rose swag, begin by hot-gluing lemon leaves (or any other foliage with similar color and shape) into the pine base. Next, arrange rose blooms in small group-

INGS; HOT-GLUE A GROUPING IN THE CENTER AND IN VARYING HEIGHTS ELSEWHERE. GLUE IN THE HYDRANGEA BLOOMS NEXT AND FINISH WITH THE SILVER KING ARTEMISIA.

FOR THE LARKSPUR SWAG, ARRANGE AND HOT-GLUE SEVERAL DRIED MUSHROOMS AROUND THE SWAG, THEN BEGIN ARRANGING AND HOT-GLUING THE LARKSPUR TO CREATE HEIGHT. FINISH BY HOT-GLUING STEMS OF ZINNIAS, QUEEN-OF-THE-MEADOW, AND QUEEN-ANNE'S-LACE INTO THE ARRANGEMENT.

DESIGNER
JOAN NAYLOR

COTTAGE GARDEN GARLAND

❖

A POTPOURRI OF SPRING AND SUMMER GARDEN FLOWERS CREATES THE LUSH OF THIS GARLAND. TO MAKE THE GARLAND, CUT A LENGTH OF CLOTHESLINE TO THE DESIRED LENGTH OF THE FINISHED GARLAND. CREATE SMALL BOUQUETS OF SILVER-KING ARTEMISIA AND ASSORTED BLOOMS, THEN WIRE THE BOUQUETS TO THE CLOTHESLINE. BE SURE THAT EACH NEW BOUQUET IS POSITIONED TO COVER THE STEMS OF THE PREVIOUS BOUQUET, AND TO FOLD THE LAST BOUQUET UP TO FACE THE OPPOSITE DIRECTION FOR A FINISHED LOOK.

AFTER THE BASE IS COMPLETELY COVERED, INSPECT THE GARLAND FOR BLANK AREAS, THEN FILL IN THESE AREAS BY HOT-GLUING IN STEMLESS BLOOMS. THE FLOWERS IN THIS GARLAND INCLUDED LOVE-IN-A-MIST, COMMON IMMORTELLE, BROWN-EYED SUSANS, COREOPSIS, POT MARIGOLD, HOLLYHOCK, SNAPDRAGONS, GLOBE AMARANTH, STRAWFLOWERS, ARTEMISIA, WHITE AND RED SALVIA, VERONICA, ROSES, ZINNIAS, FEVERFEW, YARROW, TANSY, DAHLIAS, DAISIES, MARIGOLDS, CONEFLOWERS, AND LAVENDER, BUT ANY FLOWERS WOULD WORK.

DESIGNER
DOLLY LUTZ MORRIS

ARRANGEMENTS

COMPOTE CONTAINER ARRANGEMENTS

❖

ASIMPLE VARIATION IN THE FOCAL FLOWERS AND CONTAINER COLORS GIVES THESE ARRANGEMENTS SURPRISINGLY DIFFERENT LOOKS. TO MAKE EITHER ARRANGEMENT, CUT A PIECE OF FLORAL FOAM TO FIT INSIDE THE CONTAINER. HOT-GLUE THE FOAM IN PLACE AND COVER IT WITH MOSS.

FOR THE ARRANGEMENT ON THE LEFT, CREATE THE SHAPE'S OUTLINE WITH A WILD GRASS. ADD STEMS OF CASPIA AND LARKSPUR FOLLOWING THE GRASSES' OUTLINE, THEN FILL IN THE CENTER SPACES WITH SILK MAGNOLIAS, CELOSIA, AND MORE LARKSPUR.

FOR THE ARRANGEMENT ON THE RIGHT, CREATE THE SHAPE'S OUTLINE WITH STEMS OF EUCALYPTUS AND LARKSPUR. ARRANGE THE FOCAL FLOWERS (SILK ORCHIDS) IN THE CENTER FRONT, THEN FILL IN THE REMAINING SPACES WITH BABY'S-BREATH, CELOSIA, FUNGI, AND MORE LARKSPUR.

DESIGNER
BILL PARKER

SIMPLE TRIANGLE ARRANGEMENT

❖

ATTRIBUTE THE SUCCESS OF THIS SIMPLE ARRANGEMENT TO A SIMPLE, CLEAR SHAPE AND THE USE OF JUST THREE TYPES OF FLOWERS. TO MAKE THE ARRANGEMENT, CUT A BLOCK OF FOAM TO FIT INSIDE YOUR CONTAINER AND COVER THE FOAM WITH MOSS. INSERT YOUR TALLEST STEM OF PINK LARKSPUR IN THE CENTER BACK AREA OF THE FOAM TO FORM THE TOP TIP OF THE TRIANGLE. CONTINUE FORMING THE OUTLINE OF THE TRIANGLE'S SIDES WITH MORE PINK LARKSPUR ON ONE SIDE AND WITH LAVENDER ON THE OTHER SIDE. NOTE: TO ACHIEVE THE PROGRESSIVE LOOK, PRESS THE STEMS DEEPER INTO THE FOAM OR TRIM OFF SOME LENGTH FROM THE BOTTOM. TO FINISH, FILL IN THE REMAINING SPACE OF THE ARRANGEMENT, AND THEN CREATE AN INTERESTING VERTICAL ROW UP THE CENTER WITH RED ROSES.

DESIGNER
CYNTHIA GILLOOLY

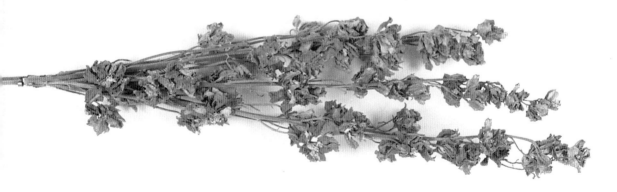

BASKET ARRANGEMENT

❖

THE ELONGATED HANDLE ON THIS BASKET MAKES THE PERFECT COMPANIONFOR A TALL, DRIED FLOWER ARRANGEMENT. TO MAKE THE ARRANGEMENT, CUT A PIECE OF FLORAL FOAM TO FIT INSIDE THE BASKET. SECURE IT IN PLACE WITH HOT GLUE AND COVER THE FOAM WITH MOSS. CREATE THE OUTER SHAPE OF THE ARRANGEMENT WITH WISPY STEMS OF GERMAN STATICE, THEN FILL IN THE SHAPE WITH QUEEN-ANNE'S-LACE, LARKSPUR, LOVE-IN-A-MIST, DUDINEA, SWEET ANNIE, AND CORN SHUCK CLUSTERS. FINISH BY HOT-GLUING SPRIGS OF MOSS AROUND THE HANDLE AND A SILK BIRD INTO ONE OF THE MOSS SPRIGS.

DESIGNER
BILL PARKER

BASKET BOUNTY

❖

A BOUNTY OF COLOR AND TEXTURE SPILLS
FORTH FROM THIS LUSH BASKET OF ROSES. TO
MAKE THE ARRANGEMENT, CUT A BLOCK OF
FOAM TO FIT YOUR CONTAINER AND COVER
THE FOAM WITH MOSS. CREATE THE OUTLINE
OF THE ARRANGEMENT'S SHAPE WITH STEMS OF
WILD AND CULTIVATED ROSES, THEN ROUND
OUT THE ARRANGEMENT WITH SILK IVY, CASPIA,
AND PEPPERBERRIES.

DESIGNER
CYNTHIA GILLOOLY

Sunflower
Arrangement

❖

A SUNFLOWER PRINT BOX AND LID MAKE THE PERFECT COMPLEMENT FOR AN INDIAN SUMMER ARRANGEMENT. TO MAKE IT, CUT A PIECE OF FOAM TO FIT INSIDE THE CONTAINER. HOT-GLUE THE FOAM IN PLACE AND COVER IT WITH MOSS. POSITION THE LID AS YOU LIKE AND HOT-GLUE IT IN PLACE.

CREATE THE ARRANGEMENT'S SHAPE OUTLINE WITH STEMS OF EUCALYPTUS. FILL IN THE OUTLINE WITH STEMS OF CASPIA AND NIGELLA, THEN FILL IN THE REMAINING SPACES WITH FRUIT SLICES, SUNFLOWERS, AND CASPIA.

DESIGNER
BILL PARKER

WAGON WHEEL ARRANGEMENT

❖

An antique wagon wheel serves as a base for this arrangement. To prepare the base, wire a block of foam securely to one side of the wheel and cover the foam with moss. Insert stems of natural grasses in the back of the foam to form the arrangement's background, then begin filling in top surface areas with Queen- Anne's-lace, nigella, dudinea, caspia, and blue star flowers. Finish with accent stems of peacock feathers, silk grapes, and large yarrow blooms.

DESIGNER
BILL PARKER

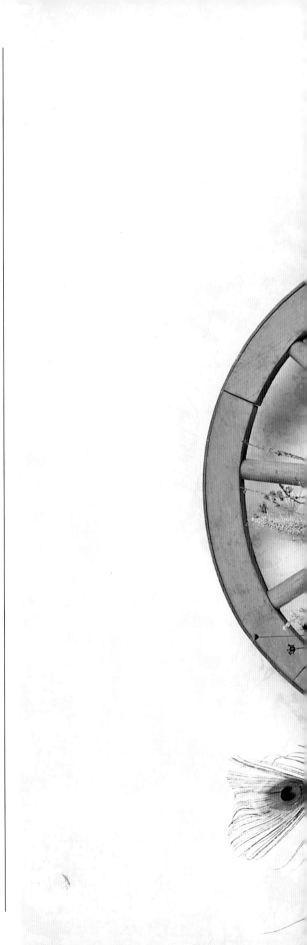

WALL SCONCE ARRANGEMENT

❖

A VINTAGE WALL SCONCE FIXTURE DIS-
COVERED IN AN ANTIQUE STORE CRE-
ATES A DISTINCTIVE BASE. TO MAKE THE
ARRANGEMENT, HOT-GLUE A BLOCK OF
FOAM TO THE TOP OF A WALL SCONE
AND COVER IT WITH MOSS. CREATE THE
OUTLINE OF THE ARRANGEMENT WITH
STEMS OF EUCALYPTUS. INSERT STEMS
OF CASPIA AND LOVE-IN-A-MIST TO FOL-
LOW THE SHAPE. ADD THREE SILK
ORCHIDS IN THE CENTER FRONT AS
FOCAL FLOWERS, THEN FILL IN THE
REMAINING SPACES WITH MORE LOVE-IN-
A-MIST AND STAR FLOWERS.

DESIGNER
BILL PARKER

GIFT TREASURES

SPRING FLING

❖

SPRING IRIS BLOOMS AIR-DRY REMARKABLY
WELL ON A SCREEN OR IN THE MICROWAVE,
AND CAN BE USED IN ANY NUMBER OF CRE-
ATIVE DRIED FLORAL CRAFTS. TO MAKE THE
FLORAL PICTURE SHOWN HERE, ARRANGE STEMS
OF DRIED IRIS IN A NATURAL SHAPE AND HOT-
GLUE THEM AGAINST A PIECE OF LAVENDER
MAT BOARD. ADD ADDITIONAL STEMS OF A
COMPATIBLE DRIED GRASS TO FILL OUT THE
LOOK. COVER THE BARE STEMS AT THEIR BASE
WITH SEVERAL HANDFULS OF MOSS. NOTE: IF
YOUR IRIS BLOOMS FALL OFF THEIR STEMS DUR-
ING THE DRYING PROCESS (WHICH THEY ARE
PRONE TO DO), JUST HOT-GLUE THEM OVER
ANOTHER STEM FOR A NATURAL LOOK.

DESIGNER
ALICE ENSLEY

FLORAL CHOKERS

❖

THESE SIMPLE CHOKERS ARE A GREAT WAY TO ENJOY YOUR FAVORITE BLOOMS. TO MAKE A CHOKER, MEASURE THE INTENDED WEARER'S NECK AND ADD 1" (2.5 CM). CUT A LENGTH OF NARROW VELVET TRIM TO THIS MEASUREMENT AND ADD VELCRO AT THE ENDS TO CREATE A CLOSURE. COVER A SINGLE DRIED FLOWER BLOOM WITH A SETTING AGENT (SUCH AS PETAL PORCELAIN) TO PREVENT THE BLOOM FROM BEING DAMAGED DURING EVERYDAY WEAR. HOT-GLUE THE BLOOM TO THE CENTER OF THE VELVET STRIP.

DESIGNER
ALICE ENSLEY

DECORATIVE HATS

❖

Hat rims provide a creative surface area for dried flower crafting. To decorate the hat on the left, hot-glue sprigs of Spanish moss around the rim, then hot-glue rose blooms into the moss. To make the hat on the right, gather a length of lace and hot-glue it to the rim, then cover the raw edges with a length of decorative trim. Hot-glue a bow to the rim and then hot-glue a cluster of blooms over the bow. To finish, trim the bow's streamers at an angle.

DESIGNER
ALICE ENSLEY

NAPKIN RINGS

❖

MINIATURE WREATH BASES MAKE AN ATTRAC-
TIVE FORM FOR NAPKIN RINGS AND ARE EASY
TO DECORATE. TO MAKE A NAPKIN RING,
LOOSELY WRAP A LENGTH OF THIN SATIN RIB-
BON AROUND THE BASE, HOT-GLUING INTER-
MITTENTLY AS NEEDED. CREATE A SMALL
ARRANGEMENT FROM SMALL SPRIGS AND
BLOOMS AND HOT-GLUE THEM IN PLACE.
FINISH WITH A SMALL BOW.

DESIGNER
DOLLY LUTZ MORRIS

MINIATURE DELIGHTS

❖

INCREASE THE INTRINSIC CHARM OF ANY MINIATURE WITH A FEW CREATIVE FLORAL ADDITIONS. TO DECORATE THE CHAIR, WEAVE A STEM OF FRESH-CUT IVY AROUND THE TOP BACK OF THE CHAIR. GLUE THE ROSE BUDS IN PLACE, THEN FILL IN ANY BARE SPOTS WITH SINGLE AIR-DRIED IVY LEAVES. A LIGHT COATING OF HAIRSPRAY ADDS STRENGTH AND SHEEN.

TO DECORATE THE BASKET, FILL THE BASKET TWO-THIRDS FULL WITH SPANISH MOSS. DIP THE STEMS OF YOUR MATERIALS IN WHITE CRAFT GLUE AND THEN LAY THEM IN PLACE IN THE MOSS, WORKING FIRST WITH THE LONGER, OUTER EDGES AND ADDING THE SHORT-STEMMED BLOOMS LAST. BE SURE TO LAY THE BLOOMS FLAT TO CREATE THE LOOK OF A HARVEST BASKET FULL OF FRESH-CUT BLOOMS. THE BLOOMS IN THIS BASKET INCLUDED SILVER-KING ARTEMISIA, SNAPDRAGONS, LAVENDER, TANSY, FEVERFEW, COREOPSIS, COMMON IMMORTRLLE, MINIATURE ROSES, AND BABY'S-BREATH.

DESIGNER
DOLLY LUTZ MORRIS

POTPOURRIS

❖

THE RICH FRAGRANCES OF POTPOURRIS HAVE BEEN DELIGHTING THEIR MAKERS FOR CENTURIES. THEY ARE SIMPLE TO ASSEMBLE AND ADD CHARMING APPEAL TO DISPLAYED CONTAINERS. (REFER TO PAGE 15 FOR BASIC POTPOURRI MAKING INSTRUCTIONS.)

WOODSY EVENING POTPOURRI (PAGE 82, TOP): ARTEMISIA LEAVES, JUNIPER NEEDLES AND BERRIES, HEMLOCK CONES, CHAMOMILE, SALVIA, ROSEMARY, ORRIS, AND OIL OF ROSEMARY.

LEMON HERBAL POTPOURRI (PAGE 82, BOTTOM): LEMON BALM LEAVES, MARIGOLDS, NASTURTIUMS, TANSY BLOOMS AND LEAVES, CLOVES, CINNAMON STICKS, FEVERFEW, ORRIS, AND OIL OF LEMON.

Cottage Garden Potpourri (page 83, right): rose blooms, petals, and leaves, coreopsis blooms and pods, larkspur, salvia, feverfew, and oil of rose.

Minty Floral Potpourri (page 83, left): pineapple mint leaves, tansy, strawflowers, yarrow, globe amaranth, and oil of mint.

Victorian Garden Potpourri (page 83, top) rose buds, petals, and leaves, sweet peas, nigella pods, lavender, globe amaranth, orris, and oil of lavender.

Designer
Dolly Lutz Morris

SPOOL CANDLES

❖

THESE DELIGHTFUL SPOOL CANDLES LOOK LOVELY DISPLAYED AS A THREESOME, AND MAKE NICE TAKE-HOME FAVORS FOR LUNCHEONS AND PARTIES. TO MAKE ONE, GLUE A BIRTHDAY CANDLE IN THE MIDDLE OF A WOODEN SPOOL. GLUE SPRIGS OF A FILLER MATERIAL (BABY'S BREATH, CASPIA, AND GERMAN STATICE WERE USED FOR THESE CANDLES) AROUND THE CANDLE, THEN GLUE SMALL BLOOMS INTO THE FILLER MATERIAL.

DESIGNER
DOLLY LUTZ MORRIS

FLORAL TREASURES

❖

SIMPLE WOODEN BOXES AND TREE ORNAMENTS TAKE ON A NOSTALGIC FLAIR WHEN DECORATED WITH DRIED FLOWERS AND SPECIAL TRIMS. TO MAKE THE BOX, HOT-GLUE A LENGTH OF LACE TRIM AROUND THE TOP EDGE AND THEN HOT-GLUE AN APPLIQUE ON THE CENTER TOP. NEXT, ARRANGE A SPRIG OF SPANISH MOSS AND SEVERAL BLOOMS ON TOP OF THE APPLIQUE AND HOT-GLUE THEM IN PLACE.

TO MAKE THE BALL, FORM A MULTILOOPED BOW FROM NARROW SATIN RIBBON AND HOT-GLUE IT UNDER THE ORNAMENT'S HANGER. HOT-GLUE SEVERAL SMALL PIECES OF QUEEN-ANNE'S-LACE INTO THE BOW AND FINISH WITH A LARGE BLOOM IN THE CENTER.

DESIGNER
ALICE ENSELY

FLORAL ANGEL DOLL

❖

To make the doll, glue a small wooden bead to the handle of a craft broom. Form wings with loops of ribbon. Secure the loops together with a short length of floral wire, then wire the wings to the top of the broom. Glue a few stems of lavender and tansy along the outer edges of the broom.

Arrange 12 stems of silver-king artemisia in a fan shape to form the base of the skirt and wire it in place about an inch (2.5 cm) down from the head. Glue single stems of love-in-a-mist pods about an inch up from the skirt's bottom, then create a ruffle of strawflowers by gluing clusters of blooms in place.

Create simple facial features on the bead with a marker. Glue sprigs of Spanish moss around the face to create hair, then glue small blooms into the hair and down around the neck. Wire the handle of a small basket to the front of the doll. Cover the wire with a narrow satin ribbon bow. Stuff the basket two-thirds full with Spanish moss, then glue in rose and feverfew blooms.

DESIGNER
DOLLY LUTZ MORRIS

PICTURE FRAMES

❖

A GLUE GUN AND A FEW DRIED BLOOMS
TRANSFORM AN INEXPENSIVE PHOTO MAT INTO
A SPECIAL PICTURE FRAME. TO MAKE A FRAME,
SPEND A FEW MINUTES PLAYING WITH PLACE-
MENT OPTIONS AND THEN HOT-GLUE THE
FLOWERS IN PLACE. PAINT THE BLOOMS WITH
A SETTING AGENT (SUCH AS PETAL PORCELAIN)
TO PREVENT BREAKAGE DURING EVERYDAY USE.

DESIGNER
Alice Ensley

Harvesting & Drying Techniques

❖ Drying flowers is one of the simplest, most pleasurable pastimes you will ever undertake. The process is the same with every technique: in one way or another, you simply encourage the moisture found in living flowers to leave. Most drying methods rely on natural evaporation to do the trick, while other techniques, such as microwaving and desiccant drying, evoke the help of science.

❖ Ask yourself what type of results you expect, how quickly you expect them, and how much labor you're willing to put into the process. If you're drying the flowers from your best friend's wedding bouquet and want perfect results, then a lightweight desiccant is probably the best choice. If you have space in a nonhumid area just inside from your garden, you may well prefer to hang your fresh-cut blooms upside down to dry on your way in from the garden.

❖ Different varieties of flowers will dry with innumerable variations. Some keep their bright colors, while others darken a shade or two. Some keep their shapes perfectly, while others shrink and curl. These variations are both drastic and subtle, pre-dictable and amazing. Experience will help sharpen your prediction skills, but some flowers will still insist on surprising you.

❖ The first step in drying flowers is the harvesting. Because the ultimate goal in drying flowers is to remove their moisture, it makes sense to avoid picking flowers when they're wet, like after a rain shower or when they're coated in early-morning dew. Blooms with especially dense petals often harbor moisture deep inside; double-check for this moisture before harvesting to prevent the blooms from browning as they dry. Late morning on a sunny day is often the best time, after the sun has had a chance to absorb some of the plant's moisture but before the blooms begin to wilt from intense midday heat. Avoid picking materials with damage from insects or mold, and be sure to harvest more than you anticipate needing to accommodate shrinkage and unsatisfactory results. Refer to the individual profiles for advice on which blooming stage is best for harvesting.

❖ Before drying, you may wish to remove the leaves from the stems. (Some people find most dried leaves very unattractive; an equal number of people adore them.) If you're air-drying, it's just as easy to keep the leaves on and remove them later if you don't like them. Drying times can vary from as little as three or four days to as long as ten weeks, depending on the method and the original amount of moisture in the flower when it was harvested. Check for dryness frequently to avoid overdrying — a dried flower feels like a flake of breakfast cereal. Store your dried blooms away from sunlight, insects, and moisture. A cardboard box with a tight-fitting lid is ideal.

❖ AIR-DRYING ❖

Most materials can be dried with one of several air-drying techniques. With these methods, the flower's moisture gently evaporates into the air. There are two nice things about this method. Once you've prepared the blooms, you don't have to do anything else. Just check on their progress every few days to prevent overdrying. The other nice aspect to air-drying is that bunches of drying flowers can become a very appealing part of your home's decor. Choose a drying location that does not receive a lot of sunlight and is not exposed to excess moisture. (The kitchen and bathroom are not good choices.)

Hanging, the oldest of the air-drying techniques, involves securing several stems of the same flower together in a bundle and hanging them upside down to dry. The stems are hung upside down to prevent the weight of petals and leaves from pulling them down into a drooping position. The stems can be secured with clothespins, rubber bands, string, or anything else that will do the job. It makes sense to limit the contents of bundles to flowers of the same type picked in the same blooming stage so their drying times will be the same and you won't have to break bundles apart when only half of the flowers have finished drying. If you have only a few materials, very little space, or know from experience that the materials have similar drying times, you can mix materials.

Another air-drying method, known as screen drying, involves spreading blooms or leaves on a wire screen that has been arranged to provide ventilation on all sides. Prevent excess curling by turning the blooms every day or so. If you want to dry blooms still on their stems, search out a mesh wide enough to accommodate the stem and simply drop the stem through an opening until the bloom rests flat on the screen. This method is a good choice when you're drying single blooms for potpourris or to be hot-glued into a craft project, and for heavy blooms that will not dry well hanging upside down.

Yet another air-drying option is upright-drying. If you're working with a flower that you know dries especially well, such as strawflowers or statice, you can arrange the fresh-cut stems in a pretty vase and allow them to dry in place. Other blooms will dry best when placed in a vase of water and allowed to dry as the water evaporates.

Wiring the stems of fresh-cut blooms can add both strength and flexibility to natural stems. To wire a stem, hold the wire and the stem near the top ends. Insert the top end of the wire horizontally into the stem for about an inch (2.5 cm). Hold the flower and the wire below the insertion point and begin wrapping the wire around the stem until you reach the end, taking care not to crush the stem or the lower blossoms. To add curves to the stem allow the wired flower to wilt a little, then gently bend the stem into the desired shape. Air-dry as usual.

For flowers that tend to reabsorb moisture and wilt or flowers with heavy petals that tend to curve downward as they dry, blooms can be supported with floral wire. First bend the top portion of a length of medium-gauge floral wire into a spiral that's

slightly smaller than the bloom. Bend the remaining wire at a right angle so that it's perpendicular to the wire stem. Insert the pointed end of the spiral through the back of the flower where the stem used to be. Continue pressing the wire through the flower until it comes through the center top. Gently push down on the flower until the wire spiral touches the petals. Now turn the flower right side up so it sits firmly on the wire stem and the petals hide the spiral. If you plan to keep the stem, loosely wrap the wire down the stem.

❖ DESICCANTS ❖

Desiccants are moisture-absorbing substances such as sand, borax, cornmeal, kitty litter, and silica gel. Although several of these desiccants have been used successfully for centuries, they have been replaced, for the most part, by silica gel. Silica gel granules are lighter in weight and tend to not crush delicate blooms. (If you're working with a sturdy bloom, there's no reason not to use the less expensive materials.) To recycle silica gel, bake the crystals on a foil-covered pan at 200 F (91 C) for 20 minutes, or until the blue, moisture-filled crystals return to their original white or pink color. Desiccant-dried blooms can sometimes reabsorb moisture; you should probably avoid displaying them in a moist environment.

To dry flowers in a desiccant, first sprinkle about an inch (2.5 cm) of desiccant on the bottom of a glass or plastic container. (If working with silica gel, be especially careful not to breathe the dust that will rise up when you pour it. Wearing a mask is a good idea.) Avoid wood and cardboard containers since they can allow moisture in. Arrange the blooms on top of the desiccant with enough space in between blooms to prevent overlapping. Place cup- and bell-shaped blooms on their sides; place other

❖ PRESSING ❖

Pressing has been around for centuries and is still a good drying choice. Begin by removing the foliage and blooms from the stems, then arrange them on a sheet of blotting paper with space between each material. Double-check for creases and folds in the petals and leaves, then cover them with another sheet of blotting paper and place them between the pages of a thick book or in a flower press. They should be completely dry in six to ten weeks.

blooms face up. Sprinkle enough desiccant over the blooms to cover the petals. For blooms with multiple rows of petals, gently pull the petals apart and sprinkle in some desiccant to ensure even drying. Double-check for blooms that are bent out of shape. Additional layers of blooms and desiccant can be added if you like.

Novice dryers should limit each container to one type of bloom. After you know which ones dry the fastest, you can successfully mix several types of flowers in one container by placing the blooms that take the longest time to dry on the bottom and the ones that take the least time to dry on the top.

Gently check your blooms every three days for dryness and remove them as soon as they're done. Overdrying is especially dangerous with desiccants because the blooms can dry to the point of crumbling into powder. Since desiccant-dried blooms tend to be brittle, handle them carefully, and use a small paintbrush to remove any remaining desiccant.

❖ MICROWAVE ❖ DRYING

Microwave drying is both wondrous and frustrating. Wondrous in that some blooms can be dried with great results in minutes; frustrating in that some drying times and results are predictably unpredictable. Several factors influence the appropriate microwaving times and how good the finished blooms will look.

These factors include the stage of blooming cycle the flower was harvested in, how much moisture was in the bloom, the thickness of individual petals, and the number of blooms being dried at one time. Then there are the complications from variations in microwave wattages and settings. Use the time ranges given in the profiles as guidelines, checking on the blooms halfway through the time range, and then adjust the time up or down depending on your results.

Flowers can be dried between paper towels or in a paper bag. The paper towels absorb the moisture as it leaves the blooms, and they may need to be replaced halfway through the drying process if they're especially wet. Avoid using recycled paper towels since their fibers have a lower combustion temperature. To dry with a paper bag, insert the flowers inside the bag, gently fold up the ends, and place the bag over a microwave-safe bowl. The bowl allows any accumulating moisture to drain downward, instead of dampening the flowers.

CONTRIBUTING DESIGNERS

ALICE ENSLEY enjoys dabbling in a wide variety of crafts, from sewing to nature crafts, as well as experimenting with new materials and techniques. She lives in Candler, North Carolina.

CYNTHIA GILLOOLY enjoys creating innovative designs with natural materials. She owns and operates the Golden Cricket in Asheville, North Carolina.

DOLLY LUTZ MORRIS creates dried flower designs and handcrafted dolls from her home in rural Pennsylvania. She is the author of the *Flower Drying Handbook* (Sterling Publishing, Inc., 1996).

JOAN NAYLOR owns and operates Rocky Creek Farm Flower Shop in Barnardsville, North Carolina, where she grows and dries a wide variety of flowers and herbs. She enjoys doing weddings and garden tours, as well as teaching classes and seminars.

BILL PARKER retired from teaching in Florida to full-time crafting in Mountain Rest, South Carolina. He and his wife, Nan, enjoy crafting for friends and shows.

KIM TIBBALS is a graphic artist and art director who also enjoys drawing, sewing, herbal crafts, gardening, and broom making. She resides in Waynesville, North Carolina.

DIANE WEAVER is a frequent contributor to dried flower and herb craft books, as well as author of *Painted Furniture* and coauthor of *Glorious Christmas Crafts* (both from Sterling Publishing, Inc.).

INDEX